Doe

poems by

Susan Baller-Shepard

Finishing Line Press
Georgetown, Kentucky

Doe

Acknowledgments

Many of these poems first appeared in the Outrider Press Black and White series
of annual anthologies in affiliation with TallGrass Writers Guild through the
generosity of editor Whitney Scott. These poems include Kill, Taking that Bite
Before Leaving, I am Ripped, This Lunacy, Pangea, Slippery Slope, Our Similar
Genomes, Pairing Off, Star of the Show, and a version of Paraclete. Countless
thanks to Dr. Lucia Cordell Getsi whose eyes, ears, and expertise I treasure.

The following poems were featured on Poetry Radio at WGLT-FM radio: Say
Loudly: I am Your Mother, Not Your Shelter, Dr. Poinar Finds a Bee, Scarecrow,
Inland, Pangaea, and The Storm That Amounts to Something.

Publisher: Leah Maines

Editor: Christen Kincaid

Cover Art: Susan Baller-Shepard

Author Photo: Dawn Bergeron

Cover Design: Leah Huete

Printed in the USA on acid-free paper.
Order online: www.finishinglinepress.com
also available on amazon.com

Author inquiries and mail orders:
Finishing Line Press
P. O. Box 1626
Georgetown, Kentucky 40324
U. S. A.

Table of Contents

III. Other Creatures in the Woods

IV. Territory

V. Bigger Game Beyond the Woods

As the deer pants for water,
So my soul longs for you

Psalm 42:1

I. Does and Fawns

A Female Deer

Doe a deer
in her muliebrity, that deer
loses when made plural,
becomes "does"—third person singular
present tense of *do*.

She's more than what she does.
That word, that one, must be heard
to be understood. She's more than a flash
in your peripheral vision.

Yu 雨

If, sitting along the Pearl River, you were told you had a pearl
of great value, and you fed her congee every morning
with your heart in your mouth from anxiety,
would you believe it would all turn out well in the end?

If, in a chilly mist, in the thousand-year-old Liu Rong Temple,
You were told to take off your shoes, on this holy ground,
would you do so?

If just outside the temple, women opened bamboo cages
to let white-rumped munias captured in mist nets, free now
to take prayers on their wings, would you believe all prayers
fly heavenward anyway?

If kneeling on a pillow orange as the rising sun,
you presented your daughter as a living sacrifice,
holy and acceptable to God, swaddled in a Snugli
strapped to your chest, if this was indeed your spiritual worship
would you trust God with your life from then on?

If a young monk hits a resonant gong, a shimmer
in a thing finely hammered and heated—
If he chants Sanskrit so ancient and folded over
that he doesn't know what it means anymore, only that the chant
has a value beyond words, still would you believe
your daughter was blessed beyond the shadow of a doubt?

If your daughter had mysterious origins but felt familiar as rain,
If you've prayed for her a lifetime, would you believe in the economy
of heaven, that the fire alight in her chest matches the one already kindled
in yours, that the will of God is good and acceptable and perfect,
which is why she is the child swinging from your chest,
though nothing umbilical ever tied you together before?

Hold fast to God, and to her.
You may have seen heaven. You surely felt it within.

Field Dressing

Deep in the woods, lost ground slips out
from under our feet. My friend and I descend
the clay ledge, cake mix crumbling away. We try
to stay upright, balancing, try to hold
our ground while it slips away beneath us.

Does remain on the fringe of these woods
never coming in this deep. Crepuscular creatures
of habit, they form feeding patterns and will return
to the same spot over and over again, even if it
ceases to provide them sustenance. We are twelve,
we are still learning what feeds us and where.
Kim and I swear we'll never return here,
never walk in so deep we can't get out.

Yelling until we are hoarse, holding onto bare tree
roots while we sink waist deep in muddy sand,
my father finds us, builds a bridge of logs, leverages
himself so he can pull us out one at a time, socks,
boots, mittens surrendered. With caked clothes
we slog towards the Country Squire station wagon,
lie in a still pile for the car ride home.

I do return. I keep my distance, gaze down at the place
where we slipped. For years in that creek bed
things work their way up: a mitten in '76, a sock in '77, a boot in '78.

In those quick years, we learn new things:
how to blend in, where not to go,
how to run if cornered, how to stay alert,
who can eviscerate us. Knowledge thrust
upon every young female.

3

Kill

In front of me, in the bed of the Chevy pickup,
straddling a four-wheeler, a doe lies dead,
tied up like Vanessa Williams in *Penthouse*—
Does are fair game this season.

Long ago Dad shot the biggest buck in our county
and nearly died dragging it up the hill to his car.
He slipped on the wet grass, got pinned between the
antlers and the ground.

Dad hung it up, draining as it dangled from the joists
in the garage, stretched from rafter to floor. I tried to
avoid looking at it's open brown eyes, as I scooted by
to get into the car.

My sister points to a photo of my father and that buck
in the garage, she says, That was our childhood,
all that loss in a carcass, hanging.

Miss Jane's Guide to Stalking

When I spot a big buck, usually at the crack of dawn or at dusk, I note
what he's doing....Then I try to guess where he's heading, plan my
approach, and stalk or try to intercept him.
　　—Ron Spomer and Gary Clancy, *Advanced Whitetail Hunting*

Don't go stalking someone's life unless it's someone you have something in common with, I mean some*things*, immeasurable things in common like dreams, goals, philosophies, favorite ice creams, and you see you two were meant to be together; stalking's more subtle and crafty, I mean, come on, you don't want the person to know that he or she is being hunted the way you are hunting him, with something akin to a shark smelling blood and going for the wounded seal right where it is cut; you go for nuance more, at least I do, or I did before I was seen in broad daylight and was thought to have taken this thing "too far" as if there is some imaginary line and "that's okay" or "that there, that's too far," or like at night being on his doorstep waiting there for hours, that hurt no one until I scared the beejeezus out of him and heard his voice do this girly sort of squeal upon finding me; I'd never heard his voice squeak in such a way, made me wonder how he sounded at twelve when his voice changed, according to his friends, and his face was covered in acne, according to the yearbook, and it—seeing him there in the dark, squeaky-voiced and tired looking like he could have cared less about seeing me, or worse, like he was *scared* of me—well, that made my stomach sort of turn on him, I mean, come on! I'm not interested in anyone, namely him, if he isn't brave enough to face me eyeball to eyeball, to stare me down, like say a lion would stare down Hemingway's gun until he was shot; I'm not looking for a coward so he must not be the man I took him for, the man I Googled until my wrist was sore and my eyes were bleary, night after night; he must not be the man in the photos I examined until I dreamed about him night after night, with me, somewhere sandy, near the ocean, and when he drops his keys and I see that his hands are shaking, too shaky to even open his own back door, a door I've seen him open a hundred times if I'm counting right, that's enough to send me on my way, if the police hadn't asked me to go already.

The Story of Heat

She forgets, "Yo tengo calor,"
Instead she says, "Estoy caliente"
then wonders, why men look twice;
come closer.

She asks, "Estas caliente?"
it's not what she means, at all.
She forgets the correct way to say things,
throws out words thinking they're close enough.

When my mother's husband lost words
they fell away like stones collected
falling out of his palm, polished and familiar,
then slipping out, jumbled and lost.

"How are you?" became too much,
no way to assemble an answer,
while he used to say, "still breathing,"
he lost those two stones too.
He shreds Kleenex, white dust rises.
This is what happens when words fail you.

Taking that bite before leaving

I can't remember how it started? As we strolled out of
the trees and onto the savannah, did I pick it carelessly
as we walked hand in hand, then with my lips on yours and
yours groping for mine, with that hunger did I take the bite
right there in front of God and everybody?

Or had I planned to take what was not mine?
It's been long enough that my calculations
are lost to me, except for this: that the deed is done.

It was cold and hard, tart, dripping down my arm, such
a fine contrast to your warm mouth on mine, right after
that bite, you eating it with me, but *my* tooth marks on the skin.

I pack and leave after that, the place lost its thrill. No more
the sweet fruit of life's tree, no longer crisp delights from
the tree of the wise, I have one child after another who can't
get along but still sometimes
I dream

...we are back, we have not gone too far. We are still
pristine. Life is easy. We have all we need.
We still have the Other's scent and luminescence.

I awake
with a start, and a weep, reach out for your
skin as I knew it then, uncovered, without all
these accouterments, minus all these layers.

I am Ripped

I am cut. My abs grooved like the San Andreas fault,
my trapezius earth-strong, delts and quads chiseled taut.
I shove plates with one hand what it takes others two to budge.
I am focus, drive. I powerlift. I clean and jerk.
My BMI is enviable. No anabolics.
Too little fat to ovulate, my body is rock,
with nothing sculpted but forged,
a vein of iron runs through.
Men move, when they are on
the bench I want to use.

This Lunacy

You ask me what I do in the dark, as in night, as in clear nights, not the foggy, lights-from-the-city nights, but starry crystalline nights, when the sky is deep and black and the full moon gleams with its halo. You ask if I think of you, just then, if you're still my paraselene? The icing that wraps that cake, the sweetest meringue in my sky? I tell you, Get on with your life, and you do, you marry, a blondie like me, go figure, gravid with your progeny. I thought my womb the only depository for your currency, that genetic moola, double helixes spiraling you and me into the next generation, but now your posterity, with her? I must get off the phone, ASAP, that quick, you paired up, c'est la vie, she's waiting expectantly, except after those tequila shots you call me, to say if you'd had your way, inguinally, that night on the roof after drinking Dos Equis, soaking up the heat from the shingles, then I'd be having your baby, you'd have circled me, diurnally, making fruit smoothies, not leaving me gestating, and alone, I glance at the crescent sideways smile, declinating, tell you, Hail a cabbie, go home, because your wife is round with child, she needs you, so don't drive your car, promise me, hand over your keys, okay, love you too, platonically, not the way I loved you perpetually, waxing and waning, my paraselene, luminous mock moon, glowing brilliantly, outshining all other celestial bodies.

Women in Heat

Grass the color caramel bakes
until each blade slices.
A breeze stirs the catalpa
so I can hope for rain, something to blow in

and she does, I know from the scent of lavender,
Grandmother's ghost arrives, she desires to set me straight,
sort me out, when I've got it wrong, which it appears I do,
as I sort photos on the porch, reading names written in a hand
I do not know, names of women whose bloodlines mix with mine
by design or accident.

"I'll tell you about the really hot days," she whispers
settling herself in beside me, in starched dress and
black oxford shoes, "We'd all be over here a' cannin'
to put things up for winter, we'd be in cotton dresses,
and still we'd be hot as tarnation. The work, my lands,
the work! We'd be a' stirrin' and pluckin' and a' kneadin'
and a' choppin' all day, nursin' one babe and scoldin'
another, pushin' away the stray hairs and the men
to make something fit to eat, to get it all done. You
gals today, you don't know how it was, how our hands
felt at the end of the day from scalding water and that
blasted lye soap."

In a photo I pick up, Grandmother is twenty, all smiles
with her best friend Daisy, caught mid-laugh
head thrown back, long brown hair loose in a breeze
behind her, free from its ribbon. "That girl in the photo
there," she says, pointing to herself, tapping the photo,
"She doesn't know what's waitin' for her, but there,
there that girl is *happy!*"

Sighing, she leans back, smooths her dress down over
her knees, "Well, some days it got so plumb hot,
we'd just stop. We'd just stop all the commotion and
we'd take a break, which just wasn't done back then.

We'd come on up here, or on the back stoop, and we'd just
have ourselves a time, we'd set ourselves down and drink
the sweetest best tea you ever could imagine, made from cold
water from down in the cellar."

"We'd just set here, trickles of sweat running down our bosoms,
we'd hold cold glasses up to our cheeks, then wait...
for a breeze like this one to lift us up and back to work
in the kitchen or garden or fetchin' eggs or somethin'."

"Ahhhh," she chuckles into the gust,
"You know, some days we'd just keep a' quiet. Too hot
to talk. Some days we'd just chatter like hens about recipes
or the church meetin' or how the coyotes been gettin' to the
chickens. Then, we'd a start talkin' about the menfolk
in the field. Sometimes we could see them from here, shirt
sleeves rolled high, the sweat on their backs, we'd be
deciding who'd fetch a drink for them that day."

"Then we'd get a talkin' about Betty, who was always heavy
with child, her husband was such a man, we all were green
with envy. He's the handsome one there, James Avery McBrayer.
See, Jim's the one you couldn't figure. Betty remarried later, after
Jim was killed in a barn by a horse gone wild, you wouldn't a'
known that. He's your missing link there in that family tree
you're concoctin'. Betty changed her name and her kids'
so no McBrayers left anywhere. Sometimes love has to move on."

With that, she's gone again, like her scent
wafts in, then out, as the locust buzz intensifies.
I bring my tea to my face, feel the sweat drip.
She knows how to set me straight, she knows
what's missing.

Cord

With Sanctus at top volume
my bones bore holes into the chair's
tapestry, picturing her knotting the rope
around her slender neck, her delicate
features swelled in the strangle of death.
A gaggle of women at my house debated
what made the young woman swing
from a noose she knotted herself.
"Have you never," I ask, "known that despair?"
They stare at me as if I had spoken in Uzbek,
no syllables they'd ever utter.
"It's never that dark," says one;
"Always a new day," says another, holding out her cup.
The neighbor's cow stretched her neck
over my barbed wire fence and pulled a
branch off the redwood tree.
"Maybe she just wasn't thinking," I offer along with
more coffee.
The dark night of the soul merely dusk to us.

When You Can't Catch That Next Breath

At the doctor's office a nurse calls
on the intercom, APediatric Code 99,
Pediatric Code 99" and we can hear
the dis-ease in her voice as your doctor
slowly rises, "I'll be back," and leaves the room.

A baby with RSV has stopped breathing,
same virus which threatened your life.
The gurgle of the nebulizer, your breathing
treatments. For months we feared your baby lungs
were like crumpled brown lunch sacks,
damaged for good.

You shred the paper on the doctor's
table as you slide down to attack
your older brother for playing with your
fire engine.

Ambulances are outside as we leave.
The baby is breathing again for now,
but not on her own. I zip up your coats
against the wind. I squeeze your small
boy hands as the three of us cross the full
parking lot. "Mom!" you say, as if to say,
"Let go!" As if to say, "Come on!"
But I will not let go,

Even at home, safe,
I put my head to your chest
as you sleep and delight
in its clarity. The easy breaths,
the steady rise and fall.

Of No Small Matter

I go to school and take snacks,
all the sugar small children can hold,
and I take my younger son, bundled up
in hat and boots and mittens and coat,
and I brave this cold, assuming it matters.

I go to bed exhausted, thinking I should
expand my mind with thoughtful books but drift
off with a magazine on my chest, glasses on
and wake too early praying that God will know
I am trying my best, assuming it matters.

I write what I can when I can, trying to keep
these gears greased while my life speeds by
and the beds get made, the cat is fed
the plants watered, the walk shoveled
the dishes washed, and the errands are run,
and I do this assuming it matters.

I have another life I live in my head
where I am not so ragged and not so frayed
at the edges, where I feature more in my own
life, where I clean up fewer messes and I write
brilliant things that beg to be published, and I
am elegant, smart, and well-toned and
I assume it matters.

Today, as the snow goes blue then gray
in shadows and the roads are slick,
when no birds are flying, and nothing stirs
except my neighbor's flag in the wind,
when my children are drawing and the house is quiet
and dinner not made because I am writing,
I pray to the God of covenant and chaos,
that all this drifting, like the snow at my door,
matters.

Say loudly: I am your mother, not your shelter

Maybe you can try to steal from your child
all the pain allotted him in this life

so he could be spared it, when it's part of his path
there to make him who he's to become to heal the world.

Maybe if you could steal it, it would dwarf something
within him that needs to grow to full measure,

the testing of strength in tornadic winds when limbs bend
but don't break, yield, but bounce back.

Figure out where and when to give, where and when to give in—
Hard to let that happen, but there it is.

Say again, "I am your mother, not your shelter.
I can do only so much," when you hear about the accident
that rolled the car, left a boy wounded in its wake.

I am your mother not your shelter
not your God, not your Savior—

I can be there, but not always, I can fight the good fight,
with you, but you'll be alone for plenty more.

When he turns over spaghetti and says "Apparently,
You don't know anything."

Reply simply, "apparently, not."

Birth Mothers

Don't tell me they're automatons, that in a moment
of unprotected passion, whatever escape that provides

there, then, millions strong, opportunity for one
to make it, a child conceived through strong swimming

through countless probabilities. While it's easier for you
to stomach, don't tell me *mei banfa,* "nothing can be done."

That the woman who gives birth never ponders the child,
like a kick to the rib cage, knee to the stomach, the weight of it?

I don't believe a child arrives un-thought-of. I gave birth to two sons,
slick as seals, who pulled on me, strong as gravity, invisible,

greater than I could explain. I know that a birth mother knows, don't diminish
who she is. I live with the life she could not have.

The Life Span of a Mayfly

is something we debate in a sickly-sweet car
full of sweaty kids post fourth of July and I say,
"They can't possibly get it all done, in one day,"
while my son insists they can—
"Let that be a lesson to you," my husband says,
"the difference a day makes," while my son's
sure of his facts, I'm not sure of mine:
how many days we have until we are not all in a car
heading the same direction, in this case, home.

Rustling

Dry stalks in a field waiting, rustling
remind me of children who are no more, souls in a field
aligned. We don't speak of them, no one does. Is it impolite?
Yet they, these gone ones, were the dreams we held to our hearts,
swaddled there at first, then real as skin and heat,
the neck of a sleeping child in the car
curled impossibly uncomfortably yet still

this is how we imagine them, the ones we bid adieu to
without ever verbalizing these, miscarried in one way
or another. The children we thought we might have but
did not, hidden, unbidden, they return sometimes, these ones

like today, twenty years later, driving before the harvest and combine come to reap,
driving with sun on the field. I think of them, children I thought I was having, before
I lost them, before women, so many women, lose children, while some somehow
survive? Who does the math to determine this one here, not that one there?

Ears broken off from the stalk, dragged into the combine,
dropped back on the soil. Inside machine separates husk from cob from kernel,
spits out cob and husk, only kernels kept.

Our bodies know, retain this, who they carried, the ones not coming
to fruition, who once held sway held dream held promise held but not beheld,
begotten, not made, Light of Light, this body memory only. I watch a dry husk furl,
carried by the wind, sail across
the field onto the road I'm driving.

Vase

The round bowl of your grief
hand-turned on a lathe

The red poppy blooms
on a gray day

I could take the bowl
and set the poppy in its place.

Beauty in the Eye: A villanelle

Kore is the name given to one of Jupiter's moons.
A kore is also an ancient classical Greek statue,
which represents maidens or virgins.

Precisely chiseled, your archaic smile,
lying beside me, our love carved in stone
I thought. We'd be together a while.

You, a beauty, solid physique and style.
Me? Clothed as always. You look at me and groan
precisely. Chiseled, your archaic smile's

such a sight to behold! You simply beguile.
I become your votary; I stand alone.
I thought we'd be together. A while

from now, I'll slip right out of this denial.
I'll slip out of those clothes, bare to the bone;
precisely chiseled. Your archaic smile

fooled me, dreams of love on a remote isle.
Your chemical make-up, the perfect hone
I thought. We'd be together, a while,

I was sure. But, that fine chance was blown.
All the things you were able to defile
precisely. Chiseled, you're archaic! Smile,
I thought. We'll be together, a while....

Settle

Then Samuel took a stone and set it up between Mizpah and Shen, and called
its name Ebenezer, saying, 'Thus far the Lord has helped us'
—*1 Samuel 7:12*

There's a bench called a settle, high back protection from the draughts, made
of oak or other hardwood, extremely solid and durable, perfect for a back hall
for when you try to lay your burdens down before
heading out into the world

or

coming home—
gotta settle that passel of thoughts down somewhere
that loose band of geese that gathers,
gaggle, at night, at 2 a.m. when the house is quiet except for the gurgle
of the fish tank down the hall, son's room, persistent gurgle
of a goldfish, now sixteen, ancient in carp years—
blind, bulbous sore on its fish face fed
by my husband now that the rooms are emptying, sons
flying out from under us as is the way

they settle in dank dorm rooms hours away with men with nicknames: Mig, Hog,
Sharky or in a basement apartment, that reeks of mold and a leaky gas line

This is where I raise my Ebenezer
still—
in a house on land with Hawthorne trees yielding thorns the size of fingers,
trees have no future here unless they've got good defense against the white tail,
Odocoileus virginianus

Here I raise my Ebenezer as the goslings, fluff and feather fly
out of here with bags and bins, loaded, stuffed, the college schlep.

Here I raise my Ebenezer
the Mama left holding the bag.

Here I raise my Ebenezer
then settle

on the bench in the back hall, once overflowing with backpacks
and soccer cleats, here! I raise my Ebenezer, so stinky with boys shoes, size 15's,
an array, all basketball ripe, and hungry, hell those boys
polished off pizzas, gallons of milk, I could not keep enough,
here I raise another gallon, here I raise my children, here I raise—
here, I. Here. I raise a blind fish and cats who sleep and shed, sleep, shed.
Here I raise my vibrations, higher, to be better in this life, as my Hindu
friend suggests, here I raise and rise, but first, I settle. I settle. Here.

Soaked in Mea Culpas

She cast loves like stones into gray green waters, into a man-made lake with a
history all its own, known for spectacular drownings—
root balls of trees dynamited out, left gaping wounds. Unsuspecting waders walked
headlong into underwater pits that record-setting-summer of '36
they walked into the water; like Kate Chopin's Edna,
never walking out.

Watching her sons become men meant, these loves she cast as far as she could
throw—emerge, bubble up, free, from underwater trappings, floating—into dreams
where she sees their young faces, akin to her sons' visages, realizes the pain she'd
inflicted might one day come the way of her precious boys. Her sons might love a
woman like she was then; feel the toss, or walk headlong into the chasm.

One lover turned mean when she cast him aside, eyes never returned her gaze, one
promised to marry her, father her children—
promised to take a daughter to slumber parties—out of his depth,
one wanted her station in life. All sunk, until they rising bloated, untethered, when
she sees a son roil, over a careless girl who has learned to throw stones of her own.

Fair Game

In March, I open the back door and my daughter runs
full sprint for the swing at the farthest point of our property.
There's nothing I'd rather not do on this March day
than push her on that swing in the cold.

Her cheeks, red tomatoes, a doe in the hedgerow watches, stays,
observes us until my daughter unleashes a mid-air squeal, the doe startles,
walks off in a tired way you rarely see does do. I watch her while men
in Kirkuk rape women, in Darfur it's a weapon of war, while men
come to these woods, look for the biggest rack, come to bag a few,
just across the fence, I hear their guns every fall.

We're female to our marrow. Bleached white bones I find each spring
in the woods are my own, my own offspring picked clean. We are the same
kingdom, phylum, class. That doe watches my offspring, I hers.
We leave each other alone to tend our own and still soldiers brutalize,
Not for me you don't. Still hunters kill, not here you don't.

Still red blood is shed, still mothers mourn their dead,
still we long for days with more pleasure than pain,
still we seek safety for ourselves and our young, still
we seek messages from the moon, or in bird songs sung, still
we long for the solace of camouflage, the safety that blending brings.

II. Bucks

Hunting Whitetail

Deer species, including white-tailed deer, communicate in a number of ways;
through a wide variety of body postures and movements to communicate by sight;
through a number of scents and scent organs to communicate by smell;
through sound by vocalization, blowing through the nostrils and thrashing branches.
—T. R. Michels, *Whitetail Addict's Manual*

How you look at other women really has no bearing on how you look at me because I am the one you say you'll sleep with tonight, share your car payment with, and care about when I talk in my sleep (but only when agitated and restless and weeping, while sleeping) but I see you sniff the air, catch a whiff, then her eye, the way you cock your head stopped me dead in my tracks, but you're oblivious, your nostrils flare, your lips curl, you cross the floor, for another beer, that's your excuse, you're dry, wanting out of your rut, by the bar talking, your hand touches her arm, pushes her away, a "get out of here" move (Or is it a "Let's get out of here"?) that I shouldn't ignore, her tight skirt and tight shirt, make small chatter until you return with my beer, which you've forgotten, you're just getting for you. I don't know her name though you do. Her brown hair around her finger, she flashes a grin, I hear you make that deep exhale.

The Cosmologist has a Dream

Every great and deep difficulty bears in itself its own solution.
It forces us to change our thinking in order to find it.
—Niels Bohr

It happens like this:
Albert Einstein tells me he almost had his sweetheart solved,
the Grand Unified Theory, just got too tired to continue.
I search the chalkboard behind him for answers.
Albert's concerned I stopped caring about the CMB—
what the Cosmic Microwave Background data show about evolution
of the universe doesn't matter anymore, nor does the Planck project
research, nor the mass of dark matter. Albert wants to see his puzzle
worked out. I tell him not through me, but he disagrees, and I say
none of that has weight or substance since her brown eyes don't shine
at me in the hallway by her office, as they did. When she holds
my hand, she's light years away, working out her own equations, lost
in the mathematics of it all. I thought I'd love like this only once—white-hot
star-like density, a singularity—this small small thing with power to blow
the whole universe into being, that sort of heaviness in this, I've seen
in her eyes, in Albert's work, where novas gleam, galaxies drift and expand
in cosmic clouds. Tell me your dreams of multiverses! Tell me you see this too?
Albert tells me to forget you. Move on. Get to work. He says your dalliances
are stupid and limitless as space. All I hear is static.

Rut

I search out my window for something more;
the buck circles my house, he's in a rut,
love's quest. A lifetime, to see what's in store,

a doe in estrus, folds down to the floor
of the meadow, not much cover, for what?
I search out my window for something more,

another buck arrives, two bucks charge and gore,
The doe runs from these who rattle and strut
love's quest. A lifetime to see what's in store,

a lesser buck, camouflaged, gets the score,
while the others battle, that door is shut.
I search out my window for something more,

I look out. There's a whole world to explore.
Soon, those bucks will be shot, trophies to gut,
love's quest, a lifetime! To see what's in store,

like her, to lavish the one I adore?
Soon it'll show, with her burgeoning gut.
I search out my window for something. More
loves. Quest a lifetime to see what's in store.

Leaving As Is: A Pantoum

If I move, I'll disturb what rests in quiet,
The deer like presents scattered around our trees.
Some things are serene even in storms,
Not bunched, but folded, waiting placidly.

The deer like presents scattered around our trees,
Why don't they lie down closely?
Not bunched, but folded, waiting placidly,
He says, "Maybe they don't need to."

Why don't they lie down closely?
Snow begins to deepen around them.
He says, "Maybe they don't need to."
I ask, "Don't they need each other?"

Snow begins to deepen around them.
I'm trying to solve nature's riddle:
I ask, "Don't they need each other?"
When do they touch and when do they stay apart?

I'm trying to solve nature's riddle:
What value is there in herding?
When do they touch, and when do they stay apart?
And, who decides?

What value is there in herding?
Should I walk out, make noise, move them on?
And, who decides?
Hunting season is over, for now.

Should I walk out, make noise, move them on—
The herd, pot-bellied with young?
Hunting season is over for now.
What I can't protect, I can't stand to see suffer.

The herd, pot-bellied with young:

Some things are serene, even in storms.
What I can't protect, I can't stand to see suffer.
What should I do next?

Some things are serene, even in storms.
The deer, like presents, are scattered around our trees.
What should I do next?
If I move, I'll disturb what rests in quiet.

Ghost Children

We were told to be seen and not heard so often
I believed it, and I believe it still;
Father would pass us in the hall unseeing as if
we had on our incredible shrinking invisible suits,
not ever looking eye to eye except once when he flew
into such a rage at my sister that spit bounced from his lips
and his eyes glazed like the sidewalk by the leaky drainpipe,
a blue icy spot all winter.

You Said It's Always About Lust

You'd choose them all if you had your druthers,
how foolish of me to think otherwise.
You love yourself more than any others...

Here I thought you'd gotten more from your mother's
side, yet you size up their breasts, rears, and thighs—
you'd choose them all. If you had your druthers

you'd do as you want, guilt merely smothers
one whose appearance elicits such sighs!
You love yourself more than any. Others

of your kin, like you, such handsome brothers
to see! Such ugly men to know. Your lies—
you choose them all. If you had your druthers,

chance encounters would become your lovers;
Women who love you can't see your disguise.
You love yourself more than any others,

which is a shame, you even steal another's
mate. To you, it's a game, you're after the prize—
you'd choose them all if you had your druthers.
You love yourself more than any! Others?

A Bad Taste in My Mouth

How could I know desertion would taste like this?
Like the buttery metal shaft in my mouth, the desire
to feel the sting of a bullet hitting the back of my skull,
to blow me all apart somewhere enclosed so the mess would
be confined?

Like the clay that I swipe from my arm across my mouth?
Planting the tree ball realizing what I thought were layers of loam
and soil, were just a cover for clay, which will kill the tree before
this season is over?

Or the taste of honey? The ripe prick of the bee's rasp in my hand
as I try to swat it away from my toast? This honey of no use to this bee.

The complex taste of you leaving, how they describe scotch:
with a finish of oak, peat, smoke—
how you walk out, shut the door quietly
as if by doing so, less damage might be done,
as if that tight pull might soothe the news.

Metal, clay, honey, scotch.

Slippery Slope

Slide slide slide down my thigh
down my side slide
until we are upside down and paired
like two halves of grapefruits tart
and pink, new like that, like ruby reds
buy bulbous and beautiful in yellow net bags

Slide slide slide down my side
away from me like all things slide wayside
wild ride finds me waiting wanting wishing
that you and I could slide and fit into each other
pieces long apart; the fitting, the knitting together
you and me so freely I leave
you freely stay under a white sheet asleep,
slide slide slide inside
my heart and there abide.

Subtle Cues for the Non-Native Speaker

> *The difference between the right word and the almost right word is the difference between lightning and the lightning bug.*
> —Mark Twain

Yes, I'll make love to you, he says.
　　What? I say.
Lie down with you, yes, I will...
　　　　No, um, what I was saying is that Jesus said that he'd lay his life down for his friends, that's what I'm saying, I'd lay down my life for some of my friends.
We can do this, yes, he says.
　　　　Wait, no. See, laying down your life *for* someone....
I can be your friend like that, he says.
　　　　Look, I'm sorry. I'm not being clear.
We can be friends like that. Yes.
The desire there, yes?
　　　　We got off track a bit here. I was talking about friends.
You wish to make love? he asks.
　　　　Let's bring it back to this friend thing, can we?
Friends? Yes. he says.
　　　　Great.
Yes, of course.
When do you want to leave? he asks.

Pop

My father's revolver aiming in the country
a pop can on a fence post, the kick back
of the gun, pushed my hands heavenward
I hit the can the first try.

What is hard is forgiveness in wake
of hate crimes where a boy takes a gun
picks out someone to kill at random
so he can feel again, something, anything.

What is hard is forgiveness in wake
of how I feel about a father with a closet
full of guns, rifles, ammunition of both kinds
the kind he fires in the country, the weapons
he shoots at me in discussions, the IED's
improvised, there, always
shot off the hip.

Binding Energy: A sonnet from the zone of irreversible strain

In some sort of crude sense, which no vulgarity, no humor,
no overstatement can quite extinguish, the physicists have known sin,
and this is a knowledge which they cannot lose.
—BJ. Robert Oppenheimer

There's nothing I seek to suck from your soul,
I've no desire for long term, have no fear,
frankly, I want to blast open a hole,
covert, a mile wide, explode nuclear
bombs underground, create cavities first.
Japan had strong winds to blow away grit,
Fat Man and Little Boy's immense air burst.
Underground's a wellspring, stuff to be lit.
Wreak havoc there, earth and all that's under,
implode, can't see damage, soil is loaded.
Rattle your saber, show forth your thunder,
create jealousy, secretly coded.
Unstable bonds, we'll form—fission—we'll break,
energy release with nothing at stake.

Interval Training

Pulls his collar up against his grizzled
chin, what it feels like to be seventy-two;
unable to get hard for anyone or anything,
balls shriveled as prunes, erections elude
him like passing clouds bearing neither
rain nor snow, nothing gets stiff but his knees
as he tries to walk daily to stop plaque from building up.

He has timed it right, the young woman running
in her black sweat suit, coughing and sweating,
her yellow hair, tossing her smile. The bounce of
her small breasts in the shampoo
scent she leaves behind, clean and fresh as air.

It's what he's here for, the nose the only sense
with a direct course to the brain, takes him back
to Beverly in the Buick after a Tasty Freeze,
her locks strewn across his right arm, his desire
for life to turn back on itself, like he's doing now,
turning back as after something he's lost; tingling
as her head presses against his skin, he tries
to take another deep whiff.
His left arm aches in its emptiness.

Doing the Math with Fernando

"I divide what I know. There's what I am."
—Fernando Pessoa-Himself

Fernando, so tortured, you couldn't speak
your mind, for the cacophony inside,
in all that dividing, what did you seek?

Who got the floor, who fell silent, too meek?
Penned by same hands, did the voices collide?
Fernando-So-Tortured, *You* couldn't speak?

Would I have loved you, or thought you a freak?
Was it a mental skid down a slick slide
in all that dividing? What did you seek

so far outside yourself? Who got a peek?
Who compromised the real you, broke you, lied,
Fernando? So tortured, you couldn't speak

the truth about loves lost, a past too bleak?
Love too dangerous a thing to be tried
in all that. Dividing, what did you seek,

as you multiplied, did you grow strong? Weak?
Reis and De Campos, a good place to hide
Fernando? So tortured, you couldn't speak.
In all that, dividing, what did *you* seek?

Herding Heteronyms

I have more than just one soul.
There are more I's than I myself.
            —Fernando Pessoa/Ricardo Reis

You're the horses we try to catch at dawn,
who shy away when the realization slides
over their skulls that we are here to rein
them in. You pull from the loops we make
with our arms, sauntering off undaunted.

Senhor tell me, who in your herd was least
broken? Fought the bridle? Caeiro? Reis?
De Campos? Or one of your lesser ponies?
Otto, Seul, de Seabra? My friend from Lisboa boasts,
"Pessoa's the best ever trotted out of Portugal!"

Best *ever*? You're a mustang, accustomed to running loose,
caged in a pen, hammering, clamoring to get free.

Once, as a child, I came up over the rise before my sisters,
saw the horses grazing in peace, and I spooked them
so they'd scatter, to settle in the far meadow.

Sometimes horses just need a good place to be horses,
to be part of the collective, checking out their pecking
order, a chance to run, with distant boundaries;
your heteronyms desired this most, peaceful pasture
with plenty of room for all.

All this Flap

When the swans fly by my window,
the thrum's mistaken for a bigger craft,
a helicopter, perhaps, the whir
of their wings heavy in the air,
fighting something dense, unseen
struggling to get back into formation
in the fog, all white upon white upon gray.
What's heavy within, gravitas of the unnamed?
Trump at the helm of this ship,
women march in pink knitted hats,
holding signs since time immemorial to protest
what should have been ours all along.
I stayed home because once I protested
and nothing came of it. Don't know
if the swans are Trumpeter or
Mute, the bill's where you tell,
the male mute swan's is orange.

Father's Care

He's doing okay.
>   *Not well?*
Okay for now.
>   *But I thought they said...*
He'll be fine.... What?
>   *It's just...*
You don't think we've done enough?
>   *Do you?*
I'm doing the best I can.
>   *For him?*
For him.
>   *I was just wondering...*
Listen, take over any time. Step on up to the plate, be my guest.
>   *Will he survive?*
Hell if I know.
>   *You should.*
What?
>   *Know. You should know! You've been here.*
What more can be done?
>   I think *We've* done enough.
Just so you're okay with that...
>   I'm fine. I did everything I could.
What do we do next?
>   I'm getting a cup of coffee.

III. Other Creatures in the Woods

Ring Neck Pheasant

The male pheasant, white collared clergy,
kept to the long grasses by her garden after her husband
Jacob left with the Union soldiers to fight in a war he knew little about having come
from Darmstadt, speaking little English, except "Hallo!"

Even when Jacob married Henriette Koppsieker—neither lovely nor dainty,
he knew she'd be strong, could endure, like women in his family, hearty stock.
The day he left with the soldiers, marching the muddy path out and away from the
homestead he and Henriette were paying off, she did not weep—

She walked twenty miles to Quincy to pay the mortgage, one baby on her hip,
toddler by the hand, breasts leaked as she walked. Kept wolves out of the cabin,
made of hand-hewn virgin timber, a chair up against the door at night. The howling
got in, paw prints in mud the next day, while Jacob fought, limped home from the
infantry

but not before she'd wrung the neck
of the pheasant, whose call in the warm afternoons, as she hung wash, kept her
company, something alive, persistent, and not harmful. Big Blue Stem able to hide
much that could bring peril or loss—to her, to her babies.

Henriette shot the bird, dressed it, tucked its long feathers in a cobalt blue poison
bottle she used as a vase, set up in the window, against the greased paper, casting
light in next to the Yellow Dock & Sarsaparilla bottles she saved, for when she
planted Calendula seeds brought from Germany, flowers that lasted even after frost,

they could bear the brunt of it. To commune with a thing, delight in its call, when
loneliness stalked her daily—then to know, it was time to kill, eat. Communion
itself. *Take, eat.* Wild like that, and free to wander. Then she looked to the skies,
feared lightning that could catch on something, set everything ablaze.

Lindsey Decides She's Perfect for the Moon

Lindsey knew she'd be a perfect astronaut—
brave, heroic, photogenic.
Neil Armstrong's face pulling a G
a rubber mask blown open, startled,
gave her pause; and all that talk of death,
a buzz kill, sitting on a stick of dynamite
ready to blow, like dating Tyler Morrison, so hot,
dangerous, and totally unreal, ready to go,
until it was too explosive, difficult to navigate,
no sense of piloting anymore, she'd heard the cockpit
stunk like B.O. and buttcheeks, that the food was gross,
and no matter how short-lived, the body loses so much
in space. Gene Cernan says re-entry into earth's
atmosphere was blasting through the gates of hell
on fire but alive. Lindsey'd been through
Ms. Mayle's 2nd Hour Spanish Class,
and came out unscorched.

Cold-Blooded

I wrap the dead snake around a branch
like the carnival man wraps spun sugar
around a cardboard wand,
only I show my children death on a stick.
The Prairie King Snake road kill,
only a little blood by its mouth, otherwise whole,
his underbelly is iridescent in the morning sun.
Touch it, I say, holding the stick, daring them
with my triple-wrapped rapier. Bone-tired
I have yelled at them, spitting all my venom.
Scales fall from their eyes about their mother.

Pairing Off

Mohawk and Tweeters, male zebra finches, wake up
with the light. Each March, songbirds return just outside
the double pane. Mohawk plucks himself, plumes
a nest for a female who never sees through to him—
while Tweeters hops around nonplussed,
lets Mohawk do the work for the both of them.
Bored, Tweeters begins to pluck at Mohawk too;
the bigger cage, all the bird toys in the world
can't keep his torment in tow. One morning,
only Tweeters on his perch, Mohawk's
a stiff clump on the cage floor. This is how it is:
*the powerful override the diligent
*you can spend a lifetime feathering a nest no one enters
*you can sing unto death for one just out of reach
*the oblivious shall inherit the perch

Catfish

My patient brings in photos of himself and his buddies
walking the Mackinaw, reaching down for catfish
hauling up sixty-five pounders that stretch more than half
the length of their bodies.

He tells me of how he once felt fur, pulled up an angry beaver
that clawed his skin, nearly shredded him, and I tell him his test results,
but still he shows me photos, thrusts them in my face.

He hunts catfish with a vengeance every Saturday, rain or shine,
right into the fall, when the water's so cold he braves hypothermia.
I feel for the fish. I get my sustenance from the depths. I'm slow,
methodical, I grow large in darkness.

Hippocampus

For perhaps it is this: a love for all things lovely, of heaven, under wraps?
A love for what stirs? Folds over in my heart, hides in my *hippocampus*—
brain's sea horse—round-bellied, majestic mythical memory?
Curvature of space and time, wrapped, rolled, encased in a bony shell?

I found a perfect angel wing on the beach, just as I was thinking "angel."
The brain can manifest? Poof! Liminal like that, whatever we think?
There are some who say,

"Why yes! Yes, we can!" I lift the wrinkly, rippled shell, how long in the making?
I whisper to God of light, God of the universe, God of the long shore line,
"Thank you!" I wrap it in Kleenex, keep it close to my plane ticket,
my passport.

When I get home, I put it on my kamidana, home altar, windowsill.
For all I've loved and saved, each memory, the ones that arise;
hook tails around whatever's grounded, and float,
right before sleep, again, suspended,
thank you, thank you, thank you.

The treetop cadence of an oriole
has me in tears;
there's a new note there
among the old notes.
—from Qin Guan's *Partridge Sky*, translated by Mike Farman

Northern Song (homage)

There's a new note there among the old notes,
Qin Guan's in exile, life torn asunder.
Geese harbingers honk news from slender throats,

the emperor is not amused, he gloats
poetry, to him, a fruitless blunder.
There's a new note there. Among the old notes,

Qin Guan lost favor, his words live in quotes.
How I lost your favor? Still I ponder...
geese. Harbingers honk news from slender throats

along the Pearl River. He'd watch the boats,
Jiangsu to Guangdong, all over yonder.
There's a new note. There among the old notes

you say, "I'm not done sowing my wild oats."
I say, "This passion aches. No wonder!"
Geese harbingers honk news. From slender throats

our desire, heavy-laden, rises and floats.
What strikes, sinks us, with echoing thunder—
there's a new note there? Among the old notes
geese harbingers honk news from slender throats.

Our Similar Genomes

The ache—
in the chimpanzee hugging her dead baby until
the zoo keeper tranquilizes her, takes away those
threadbare shreds—
                          is one I know firsthand,
holding close those I've loved until all that is left
is faded and worn from hauling and mauling of
memory.
She knew—
that her baby would stay dead, it wasn't as if carrying it
around would bring it back to life. She just wasn't ready
to give up yet.

Scarecrow

Crows can imitate human speech. And Kinohi says, 'I know.'
So it sounds a little bit demented, it's hard to understand.
But that is the message that he gives you, I know.
    —Elizabeth Kolbert, *The Sixth Extinction*

There's a message from the very last crow,
this species battled warming climate's war,
he speaks to us: "I know. I know. I know—

large mammals won't roam as once they did so—
they can't, their habitat's gone. What's in store?"
There's a message from the very last crow:

"You've unraveled something tough to re-sew."
Ocean acids rise, "You've opened that door,"
he speaks to us, "I know! I know! I know."

There's no murder any longer, "Caww, Caww,"
quoth the Raven, Nevermore. Nevermore!
There's a message from the very last crow.

Tip of the iceberg—shrinks above, below
sea floor sediment "oozes" ocean floor;
he speaks to us: I know I know I know.

Still we wonder, "Why so much heat, then snow?"
Earth's buckling, something we can't ignore.
There's a message from the very last crow,
he speaks, to us, "I know. I know. I know

Dr. Poinar Finds a Bee

Sometimes, in the midst of sweetness, we are caught,
stuck in amber, resin from ancient trees—
foolishness, not a thing easily taught

to us, but 100 million years ago, a bee was distraught
he's a new species to us, bridges wasps and bees;
Sometimes in the midst of sweetness, we are caught,

out of a Myanmar mine, the bee is brought.
A miner paid for all the amber, he sees
foolishness. Not a thing easily taught

to Poinar, a scientist, who found what he sought!
Discovery brings the man to his knees
Sometimes, in the midst of sweetness, we are caught

up in the value of an insect stuck, a body fraught
with possibility! This one provides so many keys.
Foolishness! Not a thing easily taught

stuckness, a place, many find themselves wrought—
we're glad the bee stuck! Evolution's tease!
Sometimes in the midst of sweetness, we are caught!
Foolishness—not a thing easily taught.

He did what I told him to do

I tell my lover to take my Papa's twenty-two
and shoot the Great Horned owls making that racket
near our open window.

Being a simple man, he does what I say.
I hear the pop pop in the cool night air, then the quiet
that follows, save for the crunch of his boots on gravel.

Next morning, on my way to check the horses,
I see the tatters of feathers torn apart and sprinkled
like rose petals across the drive.

Something got to those owls and tore them apart,
something killed them deader than he did.
Something smelled fowl, tore them wing from wing.

I find the black talons near the barn,
far from the brown and white down
that had been roosting too close to me.

Since June I'd heard them countless times.
Last night it was enough to make me pull the trigger,
send him out with the gun, to still that cry, that sounded like need.

"Kill them," I said to him, as he pulled on his jeans,
"It's in the back hall closet," I said,
meaning the gun, meaning "Don't miss."

My hands clean. Now nights are quiet, no call,
no answer, no rustling in the eaves. The feathers blow
across the gravel into the pasture, what's left of them.

Poinar's Ancient Male Bee: Melittosphex burmensis

This world is run with far too tight a rein for luck to interfere.
Fortune sells her wares; she never gives them.
In some form or other, we pay for her favors; or we go empty away.
—Amelia Barr

In the midst of tasting nectar I get trapped, caught in pine resin,
a suspension of 100 million years. Floating encased with petals
of four flowers nearby, untouchable. Stuck in the dark until
a scientist purchases a bag of amber from a miner in Myanmar.
I become so adored by him, he examines me every way he can.
He knows he has a real find, glows with the knowledge
that my preservation is his good fortune.

In Honor of Her House Guest

Consider the wild beating heart of a dove hit by a snowplow
buried-one-wing-out, early in the morning, before it's fully light.
My mother sees the creamy wing, while getting her paper, reaches in,
the whole bird flutters out.

Mom shelters the bird in her coat, takes it inside, feeds it water and wild bird seed.
"Lovely! Feet are so cold, but her body's warm," Mom writes,
"She must be a relative," she says, knowing if the dead will return,
they'll come back wild, gentle-bird-eyed. They'll return to her, for sure,
because she's got a pure heart, and the eyes to see, a wing in the snow.

The dove relaxes, under her care, in the cat carrier on the washer as it spins
all things clean. Still mom worries it suffers. She takes it to the vet, talking
to it, like you would to a baby. They tell her it'll never fly again, too irretrievably
broken. "Bright eyes!" she'd emailed me, "seems content," is taken out of her hands
by the vet, "put down" out of view. Such a lovely thing to lose.

Mom has attended funerals daily for the last month, while I've assured her,
"They all go home for Christmas." Her husband, her sister, her parents, all gone.
The dove in the cat carrier seemed a link from this world to the next, on the bitter
cold day she found it. Links both delicate, and strong: an orchid petal,
my 106 year old aunt, a bird's beating heart in winter.

IV. Territory

Inland

I will go over land and tell of it.
I will traverse it until I know it right well.
Ribs in my chest become rippled snow drifts in the field,
bones a plaster ceiling rippling to the edge, in the house
on the farm in a flat place, bones, my home here,
this land the bones I rest on, this land I know like bones,
know from the inside out, it's how I knew your face.

I walk the prairie where the sun sits, a seated asana,
a pregnant woman sitting stretching out wide, nothing to stop her,
the prairie stretches out all ways, by silo and barn, field and track.

Should you speak of her, and shun her flatness, tell too of the green
of the corn, the light which moves and shimmers the green, until it has a life
of its own inside your life; lighting you up there. Or talk fog settling in,
lying down, hiding distances, visibility just what you can see in front of your own
face, then lifts and is off by nine. Or the blackness of the soil, when plant shoots
break it again, awaken again, to light of longer days.

Fires raged here, ate it all up. Time and time again it grew back,
green, though only Burr oaks survived, knobby, thick, fierce
against the blaze. I will speak of the woman in the blue dress talking
by the arc of gold corn shooting out of the red combine. I whizzed by her
in the field, in my car on the highway, acre upon acre of flatness harvested.

Tell me again how you wish you had a piece of land? A hectare? An acre?
Tell me how undone you feel without it? How you wish you had space
and time to know it, how you'd become a farmer, how you'd feed someone
you'd never met, someplace you'd never been before. Land'll do that to you.
Make you better, for just knowing it.

Farm Sale Near Carthage

I.
Turn left off the hard road
and keep driving til you see it up there,
on your right, red barn, white house,
white trellis for the roses.

Hollyhocks all down the fence row,
pink and maroon, deep centers,
hairy and coarse leaves, swaying
as the pick-ups turn into the drive.

The crowd gathers early, to bid on implements.
They look over the hay rack for a bargain,
the tools with handles of wood,
golden worn spots.

II.
The plank door slides open easily
on its tracks, to the scent of seed corn
and old things thick in the darkness.
The rays of sunlight drift in
through the door, on the other side,
where dust particles sparkle, suspended,

where my father and I entered to shovel
mounds of feed for the hogs,
corn hitting the eager ones with a thud
if they nosed in too soon,
before we tossed the next scoop.

III.

In the barn's shadow in the full moon,
Papa would come out here at three a.m.
to a heifer bawling, her breeched calf stuck.

There was a soft spot in the yard,

where we were warned we could fall
to our deaths if we went too near,
it led to hell, or the old cistern.

When it rained, water collected,
the ground a bowl sinking away
into a vivid, vivid green.
Papa's domain: barn, field, cattle, hogs,
poultry, plow, tractor, saw.
Mother's: red linoleum kitchen, white
ice box, cakes and lemonade, well water,
cinnamon rolls, all things sticky.
Nasturiums stringing themselves down
the neat black rows of sweet corn.

III.
This is not the Carthage of the Romans
nor Phoenicians, this is Carthage, Illinois.
The courthouse dome looms like the Pantheon,
a marker for miles, of this town.

We sell glazed donuts and black coffee
in styrofoam cups to folks surveying the goods,
before the auctioneer begins to bawl,
like the heifer, incessant,
a wasp near your face
that makes you get up and move.

Most farmers with seed caps and butterscotch Carharts
handle these burnished things like they will
have new homes—but I know they are carrying
the old empire with them wherever they go—
I have Papa's hammer in my car.

Pangaea

He comes in unannounced.
I want to be alone, silent
sunk down in a tub with water
hot as I can stand.
"Mommy, this is your land!"
He says, puts plastic planes
on the brown islands of my thighs
and the plateau of my chest.
"You be landBdon't move."
Dinosaurs perch near my collarbone sandbars
his pajama sleeves drenched
as he peers over the basin's rim
to plant toys on Pangaea,
Mother Continent.

Laurasia and Gondwana,
my sons will shift and slide away,
oceans will form between us,
all that was easy and within reach
will not be in the future.

I remain still. I hold my pose.
I am land and earth and ground.
Then his brother calls, "I think
the frog got loose," and he is gone
dripping out the door. I slip under
water, everything floats off me.

Conflagration

Let news come, like rain, like wind, let it come—
news arrives in our peripheral vision, into that line of sight,
we don't get the full picture, just what we can see,
until the boy's bead is drawn on our heads

News arrives in our peripheral vision, into that line of sight,
bits caught in the car, in the office, on the net,
until the boy's bead is drawn on our heads.
There's no place to put news of another shooting,

bits caught in the car, in the office, on the net.
My son's pal off to boot camp, called "Fluffy" by drill sergeant.
There's no place to put news. Of another shooting,
a fighting machine, still a boy, playing with fire, live ammo,

my son's pal off to boot camp, called "Fluffy" by drill sergeant.
Rounded cheeks become hollowed, gaunt,
a fighting machine, still a boy, playing with fire, live ammo,
awaiting deployment.

Rounded cheeks become hollowed, gaunt
terrorist leaves rucksack of nails and bombs in the underground,
awaiting deployment
news shrapnel hits us, feel the sting, the sever.

Terrorist leaves rucksack of nails and bombs in the underground,
"besides weapons of mass destruction, suicide terrorism most effective," say experts.
News shrapnel hits us, feel the sting, the sever.
"We're at war. I'm a soldier. Now you too will taste the reality of this situation," he
says,

"besides weapons of mass destruction, suicide terrorism most effective," say experts.
It all blew up with a big flash of light, then the bodies, and the blood.
"We're at war. I'm a soldier. Now you too will taste the reality of this situation," he
says.

Jesus wept. "If you, even you, had recognized the things that make for peace!"

It all blew up with a big flash of light, then the bodies, and the blood,
we don't get the full picture, just what we can see.
Jesus wept, "If you, even you, had recognized the things that make for peace!"
Let news come, like rain, like wind, let it come.

Citizenship

I. Denied Entry

This is about the journey when
and where you have a place
and when and where you don't.
For forty years, to have taken directives,
must have angered Moses more than he could stutter.
How can you get that close without getting mad?
To smell the scented trees but not taste the honey?
The spicy sweet scent of things desired but not received?
To faithfully hold a people together through grumble and moan
only to find they get to cross over, and you don't?
They may stay together, but you can't stay with them.
God has granted Moses neither *jus soli* nor *jus sanguinis*,
rights of neither territory nor blood, growing up outside
his people, he dies in exile as well.

II. Deportation

She moves in the day we move out.
Her spicy sweet perfume I smelled on my father
long before I smelled it on her.
She guts the kitchen in the first week.
She strips all the wood the second week.
My parents divorce within three months.

III. Migration

Our soap does not hold
its shape and we are marked down
the chemistry teacher assumes we have not tried
though in the blue squares of our lab notes
he could have seen our Herculian efforts.
Our attempts at scent and color fall flat.
We were to have made a bar not a puddle.
Lousy soap because our atoms keep shifting.
My lab partner sits nonplussed by our failing

grade, he's ready to pay for our inability
to mix it up right.

IV. Immigration

Raven hair, black eyes, gifts from
another mother. In Guangzhou,
people point to my daughter, ask
"Where is she from?"
"Here," I say, "Guangdong province."
When I carry her through the jet way,
past customs, she becomes American,
naturalized.

V. Settlement

Sometimes you end up where you
never thought you'd be.
That can be good or bad.
Sometimes your toes curl
in foreign soil that feels like home
or a back yard can feel like foreign soil.
Sometimes chemical bonds don't hold,
and sometimes things worlds apart meet
and stick together.

Yard Sale

The soul, secured in her existence, smiles
At the drawn dagger, and defies its point.
The stars shall fade away, the sun himself
Grow dim with age, and Nature sink in years;
But thou shalt flourish in immortal youth,
Unhurt amidst the war of elements,
The wrecks of matter, and the crush of worlds.
        —Joseph Addison, *Cato. Act v. Sc. 1.*

I am both broken and what contains the brokenness,
chipped statuette on the yard sale table proceeds from all that was worn
out, bagged, tagged

Put on tables in the sun, bone china from a distant relative's set, grandpa's
three-prong cane; light, heavy, of value, of none
I am the lot left over for Goodwill

The bags holding the lot, the idea that things will sell and some won't,
that items have been outgrown, useless to you now, I am in the notion
you have to let it go

I am you moving it to the garage for sale,
in that good-bye, a glance over, a turn over, onto the counter
then into the garage bag, I am container of discarded things

Then the other good-bye when the college student buys
the teflon pan out in the yard in the light of day, buys
the stained tablecloth, thrown in with the wobbly card table

Exchange of lives, energy, substance, merchandise,
memories, money. She gets it all for a steal, remarkable
what goes down, is marked down, purchased for a song.

V. Bigger Game Beyond the Woods

Last Holocaust Act of World War II

Sixty-five years after, knowing children warned never
        to swim in this place, Vladimir Nikolaevich says,
        No Holocaust happened here; while daily he fishes this beach.

        You must try not to frighten her, as you shake in cotton dress
        in minus twenty Fahrenheit, starving, legs turn blue, still, coo
        to your daughter in calm tones, chattering teeth and bones,
        above soldier shouts, tell her:

Hold Mama's hand, I have you, this will be over soon

        You are not lost. Yahweh's sonar receives this signal, waves
        and frequency, divine bathymetry plumbs the depths,
        detects the echoes of your existence, makes note of it.

        As your shoes hit sand, a soldier hits you with a rifle, orders you
        into the water. Your daughter climbs your limbs like a tree, let her,
        while bullets fly, pull her face to yours, make her see you mouth

I love you

        do not let them have the last word, feed her words of life,
        holding her near your shoulders, your shudders and sighs subside;
        you swallow the Baltic Sea and it swallows you whole.

The Storm that Amounts to Something

Lucky, how you believed Jesus that the world
was your oyster and you the perfect pearl, that he'd sell
all to buy you; that your value did not go undetected, yet
you note how your span of time to get it all done runs
at the speed of light; sure, it was fine to hear your mom lament
her life moving south, but now you feel old,
things on the horizon you were striving for
are lost from view, you are like the two people stranded on a
highway in Utah during a snowstorm with no one around for miles
to identify you; you are in the snowstorm until you become the
howling around a frozen car, a gray milky sky pouring down; you become
cold toes and hands and faces, the breath in the air in the car that no longer runs.

Interfaths

In Barcelona, I seek langar with Sikhs, they fill me
to the brim in the gurdwara with vegetarian dishes they've
blessed. I chant near a Buddhist monk whose tones are deep
and solid as stones in a stream, water flowing over;
with a pagan woman I share meals and laughs and stories:
how we got to this place in our lives. A Buddhist nun admires
photos of my children and whispers to take note
of my good fortune. A Muslim woman tells her story of faith
which resonates with my own, while a Hindu man insists
prayer changes vibrations, just say, "Om."

On the plane over, a Christian girl, wrapped in her own
blanket, told me Christ is the only answer and I told her
my daughter was born in a part of China where Buddha
has more say. Buddha said, "We are what we think."
Not liking my response, she focused on cutting her plane food.

When a Buddhist monk blessed my daughter in the thousand-year-old
Liu Rong temple in Guangzhou, amidst the profusion of color, incense;
chanted holy words in Sanskrit, language ancient and handed down,
folded over in years and lives, the words' meanings are unknown
even to the monk who utters them, I slip and call it a baptism.
Kneeling there, my baby against my chest, the Holy One present as rain.

Bad Mamma Jamma and Her Sidekick Daughter

> *Oranges imported to China from the United States reflect a journey*
> *come full circle, for the orange had worked its way westward for centuries,*
> *originating in China, then being introduced to India,*
> *and traveling on to the Middle East, into Europe,*
> *and finally to the New World.*
> —American Heritage Dictionary Fourth Edition

You want to know about courage? I'll tell you about courage
after I eat every edible orange thing in my house:
Oranges, orange slices, orange hard candy, a limp orange pepper
in the hydrator drawer.

I'll eat orange things for the spiritual mojo, acidic and sweet,
yellow is for cowards and Courage and Cowardice
are estranged siblings who don't know shoot from Shinola when it comes
to getting along or maybe
Courage just gets along better, sits along better
with sisters Serendipity, Serenity, and Synchronicity?
Courage so often misunderstood as Misguided Monkey Business
when in truth, Courage just wants to get the thing done, wears
an orange jumpsuit with white piping,
not orange jumpsuit as in prisoner,
although we're all prisoners of something, no,
orange for holiness, orange for strength of character,
orange for rising to occasions, orange the color
that suits both my daughter and me, as we decide,
window shopping after Mexican food, gazing into the Tux shop's window,
one day, one day we will both look glamorous and fabulous in orange
long gowns, long and luxurious, beaded and buoyant, we will stand out,
not because of those dresses, not because we *don't* look alike,
but because we are so darn strong,
we are superheroes
we have ingested bravery like the nectar of clementines, it sticks to us
we can move mountains with our wills, bend metal with our thoughts,
we recognize those akin to us,
cloaked wonders all.

Where the Great Ones Are

It's after work hours and I can't cross the busy
highway when my eight-year-old asks this:
Where's the Wall of Fame?
"Cooperstown, New York," I say,
"Hall of Fame," I correct,
since we're on the way to his baseball
game I'm assuming that's what he means.
No, the Wall of Fame, he says,
"No such thing," I say, as a new load
of cars going both directions empty onto
the road before me
The Wall of Fame, where they recognize
all the people. You know, that woman Amelia,
who flew, and the Wright Brothers?
"Some sort of Aviation Hall of Fame?" I ask.
No, the place where allllllllll the people
are recognized! Martin Luther King jr., Amelia,
Alexander Graham Bell, the Wright Brothers, Babe Ruth, he says
as if there is a place
where all are recognized for what they gave
to the rest of us.
Where the great ones are, he says,
as if that will help.
It's out there, Mom, I just don't know where it is, he says.
"Hmmmm," I say, finding an empty space before
the oncoming traffic.

Union Station

It's heaven, this arriving, through automatic doors,
to enter this great hall, full of natural light and strangers with enough space for us
all. Columns connote majesty, support; people in uniform
to help you, in case this is not what you expected.

With all this space to fill, the volume of voices
changes, air vibrates with conversations still reverberating...
everywhere traces of those here before, stone steps worn smooth
with all the ascents. What a fine place to arrive, if it's time, you know,
for departure, when what is left of us, the weight of us, signals
the eye that parts the doors.

Wild Hope

Fear is a state of darkness in which the soul wanders, bewildered,
seeking help, and then comes hope as a ray of light,
and grace prevails.
> —Al-Sarraj from *The Bounty of Allah,* translated by
> Aneela Khalid Arshed

Hope is a ray from the sun onto snow,
seen when the heart's grounded, too heavy here.
There is only so much we get to know

about life's migrations, that ebb and flow.
Watch the periphery, a doe moves near
hope—Is a ray from the sun onto snow

a sign? From despair, something wild could grow?
Pushed to the edges, they flourish, these deer,
there is only so much. We get to know

camouflaged things well the nearer we go.
Spot a doe leap a fence, how her hooves clear
hope is a ray from the sun onto snow,

a ray out of clouds, one singular glow
in winter, the doe hides in grasses near.
There is only so much we get to know.

She survives, thrives, seen, unseen, despite fear.
She feasts on daylilies year upon year.
Hope is a ray from the sun onto snow.
There is only so much we get to know.

Star of the Show

The songbird in the tree by the construction site sings,
above jackhammer, above thunk of metal on metal, sparks fly
one thing melded to another, soldered in place—
for as long as they both shall live.

My great aunt—who couldn't hear a word we said—
told us, at her husband's funeral, that she caught
a bird singing far off, and she knew her husband
was home safe.

Who wouldn't believe these beauties, all fluff and feather?
Hollowed out to fly, hollowed out to withstand wind, attain lift
against drag, sing even when what's louder threatens to dampen
all spirits giving voice?

In a bush in the rain, stopped by a full throated
call, I know my aunt heard a song we
couldn't hear yet.

 A bird arrives, catches a fish out of water, or alights
on a branch beside us, reminds that all is neither
lost nor forgotten. A bird still sings, when singing
seems the least likely thing to do.

 She steals the show, this tiny one, all that song
from one so small, makes you offer up
your voice, makes you know
it's worthy enough.

Paraclete

A thing with feathers
rare bird—
conspiratress of
winged things,
perches in the soul's spire
drops white feathers
of desire.

Additional Acknowledgments

Poems take many voices, many points of view. These are original poems, but not all my voice. For instance, no owls were harmed in the making of this book.

Doe emerges with profound gratitude to

My family, Tracy M. Shepard, Alex, Drake, and Lizzie Shepard

My family of origin, Dr. Robert S. Baller, Joyce Hayes Pomrenke, Cheryl Baller Philippi, Julia Baller Biever, and James R. Baller and the rest of the crew

The Heads: Nancy E. Anderson, Julie Bell Beich, Lisa R. Smith, Wendy Boersema Rappel

Sisters and Brothers of Other Mothers: Vickie and John Robertson, Judith A. Henrich, Holly J. Houska, Gretchen Seidler Gibbs, Nora Ross Ward, Tom Niebur, Laura Bailey Reardon, Kathi Franklin, Anne Matter, Joan Capodice, Janni Favus, the Erie Benedictines

The Steadfast ArmadillHers: Teresa Burns Gunther, Jody Hobbs Hesler, Charmaine Wilkerson

Beloved Writer Friends: Ruth Everhart, Anne Wright Fiero, Judith Valente, Jerry Dillon Pratt, Laura Julier

Writing Launching Pads: Collegeville Institute, Writing by Writers, Hedgebrook, Breadloaf, University of Iowa

The voice of the Lord
causes the deer to calve,
and strips the forest bare;
and in the Lord's temple
all say, "Glory!"

Psalm 29:9

When Susan was in sixth grade she won a writing contest and the prize was a chicken dinner for her whole family. That's when she realized words could feed people, and that she wanted to write for the community at large. Her essays, poetry, photography, and sermons have appeared in the *Chicago Tribune, the Washington Post's* "On Faith section," *Spirituality & Health, Writer's Digest, the Tattooed Buddha, Day1.org,* and other publications. Her poetry was featured on WGLT-FM radio. Susan blogged for the *Huffington Post* Religion and Style sections and more recently for Joan Chittister's *Monasteries of the Heart* blog.

Susan's education included studying religion and English at the University of Iowa, where she was part of the undergraduate Writer's Workshop. She has masters degrees in Social Work and Divinity. An ordained Presbyterian minister since 1991, she's served as a pastor and parish associate for numerous churches in central Illinois, and in leadership positions at the Presbytery and Synod levels. She's been the recipient of leadership awards, and was nominated for both the McLean County Chamber of Commerce Athena Leadership Award and the YWCA Women of Distinction award.

Along with local involvement, Susan has worked on international development projects in Haiti, China, Brazil, and England. She's also served as a keynote speaker at national and international conferences on religion, and presented at the University of Iowa's Carver Medical School at a conference bridging medicine and the humanities. Susan teaches Major World Religions, Literature of the Bible, and Continuing Education Classes at Heartland Community College in Normal, Illinois. Susan's working on several new writing and voice projects. Susan lives in the middle of things, in the middle of the country, in the middle of the state. Living with her family in Bloomington, Illinois, she gets to see deer daily.

CPSIA information can be obtained
at www.ICGtesting.com
Printed in the USA
BVHW031658180419
545926BV00001B/109/P

"From the title, *Doe*, by Susan Baller-Shepard, anticipates a thicket of feminine myth and symbo[l] motherhood, martyrdom, victimhood; defenselessness, passivity; naked beauty hunted, stalke[d] violated, enshrined perhaps but never trophied, not like their antlered fathers and sons. The tric[k] and magic of and through these poems is the metamorphosis of the metaphor, suggested, argue[d] developed through a sleight of forms, often repeating forms that advance argument passivel[y] through repetition, tricksterish word play, re-castings of memory and narrative. Reading the[m] becomes a kind of active listening, hearing a kind of speaking; and backtracking, sliding off, gettin[g] lost, staying still, retracing steps—all a kind of advance. All those female survival skills of defense— the withdraw, hide, step out of the way, disappear tactics—unfold an offense, and change the worl[d] Hear, hear, hear! And rejoice!"
   —**Lucia Cordell Getsi**, PhD, Former Spoon River Poetry Review Editor, Author of *Intensive Ca[re]*

"Don't let the idea of a tender-eyed doe lull you into a place of comfort. Take a deep breath. Susa[n] Baller-Shepard is about to take you on a ride through the emotional rapids of the female experienc[e] and, indeed, the vulnerabilities, perplexities and revelations of anyone who has ever loved fiercel[y] worried deeply and observed life, in all its beauty and despair, with an unflinching eye."
   —**Charmaine Wilkerson**, winner of the 2018 Best Novella by Saboteur Awards for her novella in-flash *How to Make a Window Snake*

"To read the poems in this fine first collection is to stroll through the lives of many females—huma[n] and animal alike—with a most companionable guide. Baller-Shepard is a remarkable new poet[,] voice equally at ease with observing farm women at work, discussing Einstein's Grand Unifie[d] Theory, or contemplating the life span of a mayfly. Through Baller-Shepard's careful excavation o[f] the embers of memory—a high-backed wooden bench, a grandmother's starched dress, the re[d] linoleum of a farmhouse kitchen—you will find yourself mining the narrative of your own lif[e] That is this poet's gift to her readers."
   —**Judith Valente**, author of poetry collections *Discovering Moons* and *Inventing An Alphabe[t]* and nonfiction books *Atchison Blue* and *How to Live*

"In a few lines, Susan Baller-Shepard's poems tell stories so personal we will recognize them as ou[r] own. Stories of love and longing, of unfinished adolescence, of wrestling with death. In a wor[ld] intent on selling us ways to plaster over our vulnerability, Baller-Shepard's poems do the opposit[e] By stripping away the pretense, she does nothing less than help us find our soul."
   —**Ruth Everhart**, author of *Ruined* and *Chasing the Divine in the Holy Land*

Susan Baller-Shepard loves to bridge the natural and spiritu[al] worlds in her writing. She lives and writes in Bloomington, Illino[is] in a place where deer cross her path daily.

$19.99 / POETRY
www.finishinglinepress.com

ISBN 978-1-63534-904-[7]
5199